DR. JOHN POLIS

HARD STOP

WHY YOU CAN'T WAIT ANY LONGER TO STOP WHAT'S STOPPING YOU

HARD STOP
Why You Can't Wait Any Longer
To Stop What's Stopping You
By Dr. John Polis

PAPERBACK ISBN: 978-1-7377236-6-0
Also available in HARDBACK and EBook editions

Prepared for Publication By

MAKING YOUR BOOK A REALITY

Cedar Point, NC | 843-929-8768 | info@BandBpublishingLLC.com

Original Transcription Editing By

Susans.Servant.Services@gmail.com

To Contact the Author
JOHN POLIS MINISTRIES
PO BOX 1007 | Beaufort, SC 29901
drjohn@rfiusa.org | www.rfiusa.org

CONTENTS

Endorsements

We've often heard it said, *"I'm not where I want to be, but I'm not where I was."* This is just a way of saying I'm not maturing in the faith as I should be. Why? Something or someone has stopped our progress. Hard Stop is a quick read that identifies the three primary stops in our spiritual journey and what you can do to remove those stops. Stop what's stopping you.

Rev. Dr. Pat Polis
The Church Mechanic

Having had the privilege of being in the ministry of Dr. John Polis since 1986 and God allowing me access to his life, I witnessed the application of the principles that are written in this book. Some of them came easier than others. Some came through pain and much prayer. One thing is for sure... they have been applied and proven and can be trusted.

Joe Perozich
MFC ministries / Hope Radio

Dr. John Polis, apostle, revelation teacher, author, and friend, has the Champion Heart. He imparts this in every action of his life. Once again, it is seen in the words and heard in the voice in the spaces between the lines of this book.

Have you ever considered yourself 'unstoppable'? The word is a descriptive adjective of Christ Himself and all who are His devoted disciples.

That is not the common mindset and attitude of humanity, including many Christians.

'Unstoppability' requires the Renewed Mind. Your personal self-perceptions, beliefs, and actions you have divinely created by the Word of God and living your life in Holy Spirit. It determines your behavior, outlook, mental attitude, and victories because you live 'unstoppable'.

It requires a personal righteousness revelation. The revelation of this divine dynamic work in you transforms everything. Get to know yourself as the righteousness of God in Christ Jesus. As you develop the Christ mindset of gratitude, humility, and the authority to re-present Abba Father as Jesus did. To be a living expression of Him on earth is our privilege and purpose in power, making you and His Kingdom 'unstoppable'.

'Unstoppability' always hinges on the right relationships. A core principle of 'unstoppable' is if no one goes with me, I will do it alone in faith, but Jesus sent His world changer disciples out in teams of two. They were 'unstoppable'. The Ecclesiastes preacher said, 'two are better than one; because they have a good reward for their labor...or if they fall, the one will lift his fellow up...and if one prevail against him, two shall withstand him; and a threefold cord is not quickly broken.'

Overcoming is a lifestyle of continual advancement against all obstacles and resistance to the full establishment and demonstration of the Kingdom of God in all of its power, righteousness, peace, and joy. When you have become 'unstoppable', you are partnering to make the BEST life for humanity and BRING glory to God in all you are and in all you do.

I invite you to sit at the table, taste, see, and enjoy this meal of the 'unstoppable' that Dr. John Polis has prepared in this writing for you.

Apostle Larry Hutto

Preface

BY SUSAN L. MCCOLLUM

Hindrances! The stumbling blocks that keep us from completing our God-given directives in life. In this book, Dr. John Polis explains three types of hindrances for us to recognize and deal with:

1. Those we cause by lack of information from failure to learn from God's Word and not maintaining our relationship with God and the Body of Christ;

2. God stops us when we step out in pride, too soon and not in His timing;

3. Satan lives to thwart our effectiveness... we must recognize it and overcome him by the authority God has given us.

On the latter, Satan will always oppose advancement of the Gospel of Jesus Christ and, therefore, will always be opposed to any growth or advancement of every believer. He doesn't really need us to live sinful lives; keeping us unproductive and stymied is considered a victory in his camp. Don't let him! Read this book to learn to stop what is stopping you!

Susan L. McCollum
Transcription Editor
Susan's Servant Services

Introduction

BY DR. KEITH JOHNSON

Do you feel like your life, ministry, or business is stuck or at best moving at a turtle's pace? Do you feel that every time you can take one step forward, it then feels as if you are taking two steps back?"

If you're looking for success in life and want to reach the destiny that God has planned for you, it's crucial to identify the key factors that are stopping or slowing you down.

The truth is, God loves speed and wants to work

quickly in your life, ministries, and businesses. But if you're not moving as fast as you know you should be, it's important to figure out what is holding you back and take action.

Tom Landry was the fourth most winning coach in the NFL. Coach Landry outlined three keys to winning a Super Bowl championship.

The first key is having a clear objective. Just like Coach Landry's team aimed to win the Super Bowl every year, you should have a "Big Win" that you want to achieve in your life. Without a clear objective, you'll end up hitting nothing.

The second key is having a plan of action. It's not enough to have a goal; you need a step-by-step plan on how to reach it. Without a written execution plan, failure is almost guaranteed.

The third key is identifying resistant forces. Coach Landry analyzed the opposing teams and identified the players that could potentially stop them from winning. He then made a plan on how to deal with those players to secure victory.

These same keys can be applied to winning in life, business, and even in the church. We must have a clear objective, create a plan of action, and identify any resistant forces that could hinder our progress.

In his book, Dr. John Polis helps us see the three major forces that can be stopping us from reaching our God-given purpose. If you're feeling stuck, I highly recommend reading this book from cover to cover. Close the book, reflect on what's really stopping you, and take action to overcome those obstacles.

Remember, you are God's champion, and He wants you to win and finish strong.

GodSpeed!

Dr. Keith Johnson
Success Strategist
www.DrKeithJohnson.com

Chapter 1

WE STOP OURSELVES

> *Be diligent to present yourself approved to God, a worker who does not need to be ashamed, rightly dividing the word of truth. 2 Timothy 2:15 NKJV*

The King James Version of the Bible states it like this,

> *Study to shew thyself approved unto God, a workman that needeth not to be*

> *ashamed, rightly dividing the word of truth. 2 Timothy 2:15 KJV*

The first word you'll notice is "study" ... *"Study to show yourself approved."* If we do not study, we won't be approved, but it's not because God is looking for people to reject... *"a workman that needeth not to be ashamed, rightly dividing the word of truth."* Rather, it is because we have a responsibility to study the Word of God and to learn, so that when a "workman" is needed, we won't be "ashamed". We will have the knowledge of God's Word that we need to accomplish the task before us. Therefore, we become the number one opposer of our own selves when we do not study and understand the Word of God.

> *And a servant of the Lord must not quarrel but be gentle to all, able to teach, patient, 25 in humility correcting those who are in opposition, if God perhaps will grant them repentance, so that they may know the truth, 26 and that they may come to their*

> *senses and escape the snare of the devil, having been taken captive by him to do his will. 2 Timothy 2:24-26 NKJV*

The very first reason that we're stopped in our growth, in our maturity, in our progress toward our destiny is because we lack information. We need more than to feel a goose bump when we encounter God's presence (though I thank God for the goose bump). We need more than just exciting preaching. We need the teaching that comes from the Word of God.

What is the difference between the two? Preaching is announcing the facts of God's Word, but teaching is explaining the facts of God's Word. As we are diligent in studying the Bible, over time, the information that we receive will become the revelation that will transform our lives.

WHAT DOES STUDY MEAN?

By "study," I'm not meaning just look up the "verse of the day" or only listening to the pastor on Sunday morning. The pastor leads you into "green pastures". That's where you're supposed to "eat for a while." This is a great place to start. If everyone would take their pastor's message home, research, and study it, we would find that God has a lot more for us to get in that "pasture." We miss a lot when we only listen to the message once and don't "digest" more of it. What a disservice we do to ourselves when we say *"Oh hallelujah, wasn't that good,"* but after the service we don't remember a thing that was said.

In the Body of Christ at large, we have moved from a learning-environment, where it was all about the Bible, to an experiencing-environment, where it seems to be more about the felt needs of the attender. We've gone from wanting to grow in the knowledge of the Word of God to just wanting to experience God's presence and power. But faith in God does not come from experiencing His presence, it comes from the Bible, the Word of God.

> *So then faith comes by hearing, and hearing by the word of God. Romans 10:17 NKJV*

There is nothing more important than knowing and understanding the Bible. God puts a premium on knowledge, on studying *"to show yourself approved."*

STUDY TO FILL IN THE GAPS

> *For what thanks can we render to God for you, for all the joy with which we rejoice for your sake before our God, 10 night and day praying exceedingly that we may see your face and perfect what is lacking in your faith? 1 Thessalonians 3:9-10 NKJV*

Teaching was one of Apostle Paul's burdens, because he knew the importance of knowing what you need to know. He wanted to find out the gaps in the Thessalonian's beliefs and help fill in the holes so they could effectively move forward in their pursuit of Christ. What you don't know, you can't believe!

> *My people are destroyed for lack of knowledge... Hosea 4:6a NKJV.*

The Bible doesn't say, "My people are destroyed because they don't feel the anointing." It says they are destroyed because they don't know what they need to know.

Years ago, we had a Christian School and when students would come from the public school system, we would give them a diagnostic test. The purpose for this was to help us see where they were in their education, so if need be, we could help them learn what they didn't know or hadn't been taught yet. When we performed the diagnostic tests, we would find, for example, that some students were 10th grade chronologically, but they quit learning math in 5th grade. So what did we do for them? We gave them 5th grade math as a starting basis for their learning. This was not intended to humiliate the individual, but to help them. Unless they knew the basics, they would not be able to progress to more advanced lessons. When the Apostle Paul said that we should *"...perfect what is lacking in your faith"*, it is just as if God is doing diagnostic testing on our life. He finds out what you know already, and also looks for the gaps in your learning, that's where He provides the instruction.

You might think, "Ok, I want to learn about the plagues of Revelation," but if you haven't yet understood the doctrine of salvation, the plagues of Revelation will not help you grow to maturity.

> *For precept must be upon precept, precept upon precept, Line upon line, line upon line, Here a little, there a little. Isaiah 28:10 NKJV*

The Holy Spirit will guide us and take us back where we ought to be and then He's going to teach us right there. God desires us to grow to maturity, so we can walk in the fullness of the plans He has for our lives. Growth to maturity starts with learning what we don't know.

BE DILIGENT

We opened this chapter from *2 Timothy 2:15 KJV: "Study to shew thyself approved unto God, a workman that needeth not to be ashamed, rightly dividing the word of truth."* The word "study" here means "be diligent." What does it mean to be diligent? It means start something and finish it. We can be all hyped up about a message our pastor preached or about a passage we read in the Bible, and as Luke 8:13 states "*we receive the Word with joy,*", thinking we are going to study that out, but somehow, we forget about it, we don't continue with it, and we miss a season of teaching in our life that God was trying to bring to us.

Be diligent and study the Word of God. Get a good study Bible and commentaries, Bible software for your computer, phone, or tablet. Dig out the deeper truths in that message or passage that got you so excited. Start breaking down the Greek and Hebrew words and study about the authorship of a book; who they were writing to and the purpose behind the book. Study the Word of God...don't just read it, study it.

KEEP PACE

I want to encourage you that every time there is an opportunity to learn at your local church, if it is humanly possible, get your note pad and your Bible and plan to be there to study the Word of God. Whether it is a Sunday morning, evening or any day through the week, if you can be there, be there to learn the Word of God. Take classes in the church seriously. This might sound really basic, but it's a big problem because people are more experience and excitement-oriented than they are education-oriented in growing and learning. An experience will not get you through this life; it's what you've learned from God's Word that's going to get you through all trials you face.

One reason people fall out of the church God called them to is because they are not growing or keeping pace with where God is leading the ministry. They are not "eating what's being fed". A friend of mine said, *"Where He leads me, I'll follow; what He feeds me, I'll swallow."* You must grow with your church.

Your pastors are growing, your leaders are growing; they're feeding, they're studying, and the corporate destiny of your church is progressing. But, if you don't stay in sync with it, eventually you're going to be out of sync and then you're going to feel as if you don't fit anymore. When this happens, you're going to move toward the back door; you're going to unplug and disengage from the vision, and think, *"Well, my season here is over."* But the reality is you stopped growing with everyone else.

For clarity, let's take a brief look into the topic of "seasons". What does a season consist of? A season is composed of preparing the ground, planting seeds, rainfall, something grows, then a harvest. If you're going to claim a season is over, have you been through all those steps? I understand how we use the terminology, but I don't think it's correct. When God is finished with us at a ministry, it's because He's accomplished His purpose there in our life. Not only will you know that, but your leadership will know that too.

When it's time to move to the next thing, you should never just go out, you should be sent out. When you are sent out, it's because something is finished, and God is ready to move you on to the next thing. This usually means a time of promotion, or God taking you to a place of higher authority and responsibility. When you go out, you are usually going by yourself and you end up wandering in the wilderness, because you never learned what God was wanting you to learn in the first place.

Here is a simple analogy about staying connected. If you were a grape, you have to hang with the cluster. A grape that falls off the cluster becomes a what? A raisin. You'll get dried up; therefore, to continue to grow you must stay connected with the group that is connected to the vine; grapes hang together.

> *Thus says the Lord: "As the new wine is found in the cluster..." Isaiah 65:8 NKJV.*

It comes in a corporate setting where all the grapes are hung together on the same vine; that's where the corporate anointing comes and the move of God begins.

Make the decision that you are going to become a student of the Word of God and are going to be taught. When my pastor speaks, we must take the attitude of "*God is speaking this word for us here in the church,*" I'm going to go home and "graze" (study, contemplate, "digest") in that word for a while and not just forget it.

HOW TO RECEIVE REVELATION KNOWLEDGE

Let's take "study" a step further. There is a process for unlocking "revelation" from the Written Word of God that will release the power of the Word into our lives resulting in "transformation." Any condition or situation we are facing can be "transformed" by the revelation knowledge of God's Word when it is applied to our lives,

> *But be doers of the word, and not hearers only, deceiving yourselves. 23 For if anyone is a hearer of the word and not a doer, he is like a man observing his natural face in a mirror; 24 for he observes himself, goes away, and immediately forgets what kind of man he was. 25 But he who looks into the perfect law of liberty and continues in it, and is not a forgetful hearer but a doer of the work, this one will be blessed in what he does. James 1:22-25 NKJV*

One great Bible teacher has pointed out that, *"faith is that which accompanies knowledge."* In other words when you get the knowledge from the

Spirit of God, you get the faith, like "*wet goes with water.*" When you get the water, you get the wet also, you can't separate the two.

I have experienced the transforming power of God's Word on various levels, including my health, finances, family and ministry. Let me give you an example or two from my own life experiences before I show you the process of obtaining "revelation and power" from the Word of God.

My personal health has been transformed solely by the power in God's Word time and again without the aid of medical science. I am grateful for the medical profession that God has provided, primarily for those who don't have a Covenant with God Almighty, but I have discovered that God has agreed to take care of my body if I follow the instructions found in the Bible.

> *and said, "If you diligently heed the voice of the Lord your God and do what is right in His sight, give ear to His commandments*

and keep all His statutes, I will put none of the diseases on you which I have brought on the Egyptians. For I am the Lord who heals you." Exodus 15:26 NKJV

"So you shall serve the Lord your God, and He will bless your bread and your water. And I will take sickness away from the midst of you. 26 No one shall suffer miscarriage or be barren in your land; I will fulfill the number of your days." Exodus 23:25-26 NKJV

I was born with a heart condition and suffered Rheumatic Fever as a young child. I outgrew the heart murmur and was able to join the USMC after High School and served in Vietnam in 1969. After my short stint in the military (due to combat injuries), I had a several year period of drug and alcohol abuse that affected my heath and aggravated the old heart condition. Then I became a pastor and the stress of ministry put pressure on my heart until I began having a series of heart issues that left me weak and unable to climb three stairs without struggling to breath, I was just in my mid-thirties at the time. I decided I would trust God only with my need for healing and began meditation of the scriptures relating to my Covenant of Health. Faith was growing and knowledge was increasing until my faith reached a level that enabled me to believe "I WAS HEALED" (*past tense*) regardless of the symptoms in my body.

We have only learned to live by our "five senses" but I discovered that we have a "sixth sense" as well, called "believing with the heart." (*Listen to Dr. John's message called* ***The Sixth Sense*** *on the free Faith Church App. Search your app store for "****Faith Church INT****" or you can scan the QR code.)*

> *For with the heart one believes unto righteousness, and with the mouth confession is made unto salvation. Romans 10:10 NKJV*

By simply "acting on the revealed knowledge" I had received through meditation of the scriptures, the power in God's Word was released into my spirit resulting in my body being healed and a new heart received. At the time of this writing, I am 72 years old and in very good health, having recently achieved a Black Belt in the martial art of Hapkido. I say all this to the glory and praise of God Almighty. I have no intention of retiring from ministry, but look forward to many more years of productivity in my calling as an International Apostolic Leader. As I meditated on the scriptures, God spoke this definition to me that has worked each time I employ it, no matter the situation or condition at hand,

"FAITH, OR ACTING ON THE WORD OF GOD WITHOUT HAVING EXTRA EVIDENCE IN THE FIVE SENSES, WILL RELEASE THE POWER IN GOD'S WORD INTO YOUR SPIRIT."

Notice that God works through our spirit man

first and power is released through "words and actions" that correspond with the Word. It works all the time because,

> *"God is not a man, that He should lie, Nor a son of man, that He should repent. Has He said, and will He not do? Or has He spoken, and will He not make it good?" Numbers 23:19 NKJV*

Another example of the power of God's Word working took place in the local church I currently serve as Senior Leader. I began pastoring in West Virginia in 1980 with a small church of approximately 40 to 50 elderly people, on Sunday morning. We grew to a regular attendance to average 340 people by 1991, most of the folks were born again and baptized in our ministry. Of course there are always transplants from other churches and dechurched people coming back to the House of God.

I was led to install another pastor and move to

the Carolinas where we planted two more churches. Unfortunately, the leadership I left in charge had some personal problems that affected the church and attendance had dwindled to about 50 people on Sunday. God sent me back to WV in 2006 to take the helm again and bring about a recovery of the church. It was a very dismal time in my life, the town where the church is located is not large and everyone knew that our once thriving church was on the verge of closing its doors. I wanted to close the doors, sell the property and move on to continue ministry in other locations. Someone has correctly stated, *"It's easier to make a baby, than to raise the dead."* That was exactly how I felt at the time, but God had other plans and I was not at liberty to do anything but "dig in" and start over again. As I was walking and praying in the sanctuary one day seeking God for answers on how to get things moving again, He spoke these words to my spirit;

"Move the platform to the opposite side of

the sanctuary because I am going to turn this church around."

It was a prophetic word that required a prophetic act which we did immediately. I called some men and we took the platform apart and rebuilt it on the opposite side of the room as God instructed. Well, it didn't take long for the Spirit of God to start moving in a fresh anointing that was attracting people again to our services. I changed the church name for rebranding purposes, did a bit of cosmetic upgrades and just "preached, prayed and prophesied" to the new attendees. The power of the Word worked in this situation and our church has become a leading church in the community again, with TV, Radio, Publications, World Missions, Community Projects, and more. There is no situation or condition that cannot be transformed by the Word of God. Now, here is the process of releasing the power of the Word into your life and needs. It begins with,

- INFORMATION - The written Word.
- MEDITATION - Turning the Word over in our minds which results in
- REVELATION - The spiritual understanding of the Word, this releases
- IMPARTATION - The creative power is released with the revelation, bringing the
- TRANSFORMATION - Your need is met.

This is the process God gave me many years ago that works for 'WHOSOEVER WILL."

Chapter 2

GOD STOPS US

Or do you think that the Scripture says in vain, "The Spirit who dwells in us yearns jealously"? 6 But He gives more grace. Therefore He says: "God resists the proud, But gives grace to the humble." 7 Therefore submit to God. Resist the devil and he will flee from you. James 4:5-7 NKJV.

"God resists the proud, but He gives grace" to who? The humble! What we're addressing here is to stop whatever is stopping you. First we have seen from

scripture that if we're not learning and growing in the knowledge of God's Word, then we're stopping ourselves. Second, if you and I don't learn humility in our life, then God resists us. God stops us right where we are. There are many people that blame Satan when it is God who has put the brakes on in their life. They can't seem to go anywhere; they will try this and that; they are trying to break out of a rut, but God is resisting them and nothing they do works.

> *Likewise you younger people, submit yourselves to your elders. Yes, all of you be submissive to one another, and be clothed with humility, for "God resists the proud, But gives grace to the humble." 6 Therefore humble yourselves under the mighty hand of God, that He may exalt you in due time,*
> *1 Peter 5:5-6 NKJV*

Notice in this scripture, it is God who *"resists the proud, but gives grace to the humble."* Humility is key!

HUMILITY IN THE LIFE OF JESUS

His parents went to Jerusalem every year at the Feast of the Passover. 42 And when He was twelve years old, they went up to Jerusalem according to the custom of the feast. 43 When they had finished the days, as they returned, the Boy Jesus lingered behind in Jerusalem. And Joseph and His mother did not know it; 44 but supposing Him to have been in the company, they went a day's journey, and sought Him among their relatives and acquaintances. 45 So when they did not find Him, they returned to Jerusalem, seeking Him. 46 Now so it was that after three days they found Him in the temple, sitting in the midst of the teachers, both listening to them and asking them questions. 47 And all who heard Him were astonished at His understanding and answers. 48 So when they saw Him, they were amazed; and His mother said to Him, "Son, why have You done this to us? Look, Your father and I

> *have sought You anxiously." 49 And He said to them, "Why did you seek Me? Did you not know that I must be about My Father's business?" 50 But they did not understand the statement which He spoke to them. 51 Then He went down with them and came to Nazareth, and was [b]subject to them, but His mother kept all these things in her heart. 52 And Jesus increased in wisdom and stature, and in favor with God and men. Luke 2:41-52 NKJV*

Typically, when we read this story, we get excited and think, "Wow, Jesus was a superstar when He was only 12, the boy wonder. Even at a young age, He could "wow" the doctors and the lawyers in the temple.

The truth is, even though Jesus had an understanding of God's Word, He was still a boy who needed to learn humility. These verses tell us of how He stayed behind in Jerusalem and didn't tell His parents where He was going. He kind of broke away and acted independently of authority. He acted prematurely.

As I thought about this one day, the Holy Spirit brought something to my attention. He said, *"Jesus was a Jewish boy under the law."* He left His parents by taking off and leaving them without permission or letting them know where He was going. As a parent, that wouldn't work at your house, right? No matter how much of a child protégé you might have, that wouldn't be acceptable.

Some people have gotten angry at me for teaching this, because they say, *"Now Jesus couldn't have manifested any independent spirit."* Yet, scripture informs...

> *For we do not have a High Priest who cannot sympathize with our weaknesses, but was in all points tempted as we are, yet without sin. Hebrews 4:15 NKJV*

Jesus was tempted in all ways, yet did not sin. In the Luke 2 scripture, He was tempted to break away from authority and do His own thing. He may have thought He was ready to begin His ministry. He may have thought He was ready because He had some revelation and understanding. Being 12 years of age, it was His Bar Mitzvah time when it is said in Jewish tradition that, "you're now a man". Jesus may have thought, "Well, I guess it's time for me to break away from mom and dad and go do what God called me to do without letting them know anything about it." When, in fact, Jesus was being tempted to do what a lot of us do – break away from authority and go on our own and act independently because we have sized ourselves up and we determined we are ready to go, and that we don't need anybody to affirm us...self-appointed. There are many people who are out among the church body who are self-appointed. They have a revelation from God and they think they're ready to go when they haven't got the approval or affirmation of anybody in authority. They affirmed and approved themselves because God has given them some kind of revelation knowledge from His Word. The fact was, Jesus wasn't ready to go. He didn't know what His preparation was going to require any more than you or I do. That's why we can't be a "*law unto oneself*" and launch ourselves into ministry, because we don't know when we're ready. We need a spiritual father or mother in our life to confirm our readiness. Jesus broke away from His earthly mom and dad; He was tempted to operate in an Independent Spirit (not influenced or "covered" by other people), which would lead Him to sinful pride.

I believe Jesus was on the precipice of crossing the line into sin, being tempted by high-mindedness. Was He temped on all points? Does the Bible say that? **Yes!** That means He had to be tempted with pride at some point, though we don't like to think about Jesus that way. He was tempted with pride and high-mindedness, thinking "I'm ready to go".

Here is Jesus, broken away prematurely, and

when His earthly mom and dad catch up with Him, and say *"where have you been? We've been searching and crying for three days; we thought a lion or something ate you; you shouldn't do these things. You're only 12 years old, you're still under the law."* Then Jesus replied with what I believe was a little bit of an arrogant comment, *"Well, mom and dad, you should have known where I was. Did you not know that I must be about My Father's business?"* Jesus kind of got back in His earthly mom and dad's face. We know it's not proper for kids to correct their mom and dad. Here is what cinches it for me, that He was being tempted with pride – look at verse 51,

> *Then He went down with them and came to Nazareth, and was **subject** to them, but His mother kept all these things in her heart. Luke 2:51 NKJV (emphasis added)*

Up to that point, He was not being subject to them. After this occurred, He made Himself obedient to become subject to them, meaning "to make obedient to," that's what the word 'subject" means.

I believe He realized how dangerously close He was to crossing the line; *"He was tempted in all points"* just like as we are, and when He realized what was going on, He said to Himself *"I'm going back home, I'll never do that again, I'm going to get back under the authority of My earthly mom and dad!"*

> *Pride goes before destruction, And a haughty spirit before a fall. Proverbs 16:18 NKJV*

Satan knew that he could have had Jesus right in that moment had Jesus not gone back home and made Himself subject to the authority over Him; He would have crossed the line and been in sin. If that occurred, we wouldn't have ever had a Savior; we'd all still be lost in our sin. Jesus learned humility.

THE BENEFITS OF HUMILITY

There were three things that happened when He went back and subjected Himself to authority in His life. The Bible states,

> *And Jesus increased in wisdom and stature, and in favor with God and men. Luke 2:52 NKJV*

Jesus made Himself subject to the God given authority in His life and from there He increased in wisdom, stature, and in favor!

There are few that choose to walk in the level of humility that Jesus walked in. Think about this as a leader, how many people do you see come back and say, *"I was premature, I shouldn't have left"*? Pride gets in the way and keeps them from saying it. God bless that person who comes back and says, *"I shouldn't have left. I was premature because I had some revelation knowledge, and when someone praised me for what I knew, I got into pride thinking I knew more than my leader."*

When someone is sharing what they know prematurely, a mature person will look and say, *"Oh this person ought to be keeping quiet, they're not ready yet,"* but a religious person might say *"Oh, you ought to preach tomorrow; wonder why the pastor is not recognizing your gift?"* But staying in humility by being subject to the authority God has put in our life will always be the path to promotion. When Jesus went back home and He made Himself subject, He recovered from this temptation to be independent from authority in His life. He humbled Himself. He became obedient to the authorities God had set in His life, which were Mary and Joseph. And because of this repositioning, He put Himself in a position to grow and increase. Had He not put Himself in the position to grow and increase, what might have happened? He would not have grown or increased anymore; He would have stayed at that level of revelation, and He wouldn't have had enough maturity and wisdom to carry out His assignment here on earth. He would never have been released into His purpose (ministry). We must learn humility and stick with "our parents" until the day of release comes and that day will come.

> *When all the people were baptized, it came to pass that Jesus also was baptized; and while He prayed, the heaven was opened. 22 And the Holy Spirit descended in bodily form like a dove upon Him, and a voice came from heaven which said, "You are My beloved Son; in You I am well pleased."*
> *Luke 3:21-22 NKJV*

When Jesus was 30 years old, He was baptized by John in the river, and a voice from heaven opened and spoke. God said, *"Okay, I'm pleased."* What was He pleased with here? He was pleased with His maturity and wisdom. He was pleased with what happened in Jesus from age 12 to 30; how He grew and matured while under authority. God said, *"It's time for You to be heard, this is My beloved Son in whom I am well pleased. It's time for you to be heard!"*

There is a time for you to be heard. You could go out preaching before it's time, and the only people to gain from your preaching will be a few religious folks that are going to "scratch your back" because they have a different agenda.

The number one way we are stopped is when we stop ourselves, because we don't know what we need to know. The second way is when God opposes us because we lack humility, or we are breaking away from authority and acting independently premature. When God opposes us, nothing will work!

Chapter 3

SATAN ATTEMPTS TO STOP US

So far we have looked at what is stopping us as followers of Christ. The first way we are stopped is when we stop ourselves because we don't know what we need to know. The second way is when God opposes us because we lack humility. The third way is when the devil is trying to stop us

THE DEVIL TRIED TO STOP JESUS

Now when He got into a boat, His disciples followed Him. 24 And suddenly a great

> *tempest arose on the sea, so that the boat was covered with the waves. But He was asleep. 25 Then His disciples came to Him and awoke Him, saying, "Lord, save us! We are perishing!" 26 But He said to them, "Why are you fearful, O you of little faith?" Then He arose and rebuked the winds and the sea, and there was a great calm. Matthew 8:13-26 NKJV*

These scriptures describe where Jesus was on an assignment from God to cross the lake and cast out the devil from the Demoniac of Gadara. As we see in Luke's account of this deliverance, Jesus would then commission that man as an evangelist by sending him back to win his town for Jesus.

> *Now the man from whom the demons had departed begged Him that he might be with Him. But Jesus sent him away, saying, 39 "Return to your own house, and tell what great things God has done for you." And he went his way and proclaimed throughout the whole city what great*

things Jesus had done for him. Luke 8:38-39 NKJV

Jesus was going to the other side of the lake because there was a demonic territorial stronghold over there that He had the anointing to destroy and break. Satan knew Jesus was coming so he sent out a storm, which was a demonic power released to kill Jesus in the middle of the lake.

How do we know it was a demonic power behind the storm? The Bible reads Jesus *"rebuked the winds and the sea."* The word "rebuke" is a Greek word "Epitimao" which is the same word Jesus used when He rebuked the deaf and dumb spirits and cast demons out of people.

We see this when Jesus rebuked the demon in the epileptic boy.

And when they had come to the multitude, a man came to Him, kneeling down to Him and saying, 15 "Lord, have mercy on my son, for he is an epileptic and suffers

> *severely; for he often falls into the fire and often into the water. 16 So I brought him to Your disciples, but they could not cure him." 17 Then Jesus answered and said, "O faithless and perverse generation, how long shall I be with you? How long shall I bear with you? Bring him here to Me." 18 And Jesus* ***rebuked*** *the demon, and it came out of him; and the child was cured from that very hour. 19 Then the disciples came to Jesus privately and said, "Why could we not cast it out?"Matthew 17:14-19 NKJV (emphasis added)*

The same word is used by all who recorded this deliverance.

> *Then Jesus* ***rebuked*** *the unclean spirit, healed the child, and gave him back to his father. Luke 9:42 NKJV (emphasis added)*

> *When Jesus saw that the people came running together, He* ***rebuked*** *the unclean spirit, saying to it, "Deaf and dumb spirit, I command you, come out of him and enter*

him no more!" Mark 9:25 NKJV (emphasis added)

Jesus used the same word, "Epitimao" (rebuke) to rebuke that storm, because He was talking to the devil behind that storm.

The only time Satan is really going to resist you is when you're in the will of God. The rest of the time, it's me opposing myself, or God resisting me. But when I have been sent by God on a mission and divine assignment, Satan will come against me and try to stop me, but we have authority in Jesus' name, which is the answer in such a situation.

THE DEVIL TRIED TO STOP PAUL

Our enemy will try to stop us in our walk of fellowship with God, and work in the Kingdom. At the very least, he will attempt to "hinder us" as Paul said in 1 Thessalonians 2,

But we, brethren, having been taken away from you for a short time in presence, not

> *in heart, endeavored more eagerly to see your face with great desire. 18 Therefore we wanted to come to you—even I, Paul, time and again—but Satan hindered us. 1 Thessalonians 2:17-18 NKJV*

The word hindered is from the Greek word, "egkopto" which means "to cut into", "impede", "detain". "To be tedious unto."

The devil stirred up people against Paul in many cities where he preached the Gospel and attempted to end his life several times. Just like he did to Jesus during His earth walk.

> *Are they ministers of Christ?* (Speaking of those who were saying Paul was a false apostle) *—I speak as a fool—I am more: in labors more abundant, in stripes above measure, in prisons more frequently, in deaths often. 24 From the Jews five times I received forty stripes minus one. 25 Three times I was beaten with rods; once I was stoned; three times I was shipwrecked; a*

> *night and a day I have been in the deep; 26 in journeys often, in perils of waters, in perils of robbers, in perils of my own countrymen, in perils of the Gentiles, in perils in the city, in perils in the wilderness, in perils in the sea, in perils among false brethren; 27 in weariness and toil, in sleeplessness often, in hunger and thirst, in fastings often, in cold and nakedness. 2 Corinthians 11:23-27 NKJV (note added)*

Satan and his emissaries will "form weapons" to "steal, kill and destroy" God's people, especially those who have answered the call of God to serve in the supernatural ministry of the Church. But we are assured that **even if Satan starts a fight with the believer, the child of God will finish it and destroy the works of the devil.** The Apostle Paul is a great example to us today of a "victorious warrior" in God's Army. He faced every obstacle and demonic attack that we can imagine, but none of them overcame him.

Therefore I take pleasure in infirmities, in reproaches, in needs, in persecutions, in distresses, for Christ's sake. For when I am weak, then I am strong. 2 Corinthians 12:10 NKJV

"No weapon formed against you shall prosper, And every tongue which rises against you in judgment You shall condemn. This is the heritage of the servants of the Lord, And their righteousness is from Me," Says the Lord. Isaiah 54:17 NKJV

At the close of a glorious career in serving Christ, Paul could make the following statement for all believers to take to heart in 2 Timothy 4,

For I am already being poured out as a drink offering, and the time of my departure is at hand. 7 I have fought the good fight, I have finished the race, I have kept the faith. 8 Finally, there is laid up for me the crown of righteousness, which the Lord, the righteous Judge, will give to

> *me on that Day, and not to me only but also to all who have loved His appearing. 2 Timothy 4:6-8 NKJV*

Paul was not victorious because he was an "apostle" but because he had knowledge of the authority he shared with the Risen Lord. Paul exercised faith in the grace of God that is available to all believers "in Christ."

> *And He said to me, "My grace is sufficient for you, for My strength is made perfect in weakness." Therefore most gladly I will rather boast in my infirmities (inability in self to defeat the enemy), that the power of Christ may rest upon me. 2 Corinthians 12:9 NKJV*

Like Apostle Paul, (not equating myself with him, of course) I have had some "close encounters" of the demonic kind over the years in ministry when Satan was attempting to stop me from obeying the call and vision God had given me. As

I stated earlier, the enemy doesn't waste time on those who are not a threat to his kingdom, but all the bells go off in Hell when a believer gets serious about fulfilling the assignment on their life. When you walk in your God given assignment, you will walk in the power of God because the "anointing is on the assignment." When Satan recognizes the anointing of God in manifestation, he knows that he must get at the vessel carrying the anointing and put a stop to the damage being done to the demonic realm.

> *It shall come to pass in that day That his burden will be taken away from your shoulder, And his yoke from your neck, And the yoke will be destroyed because of the anointing oil. Isaiah 10:27 NKJV*

> *"The Spirit of the Lord is upon Me, Because He has anointed Me To preach the gospel to the poor; He has sent Me to heal the brokenhearted, To proclaim liberty to the captives And recovery of sight to the blind,*

> *To set at liberty those who are oppressed;" Luke 4:18 NKJV*

THE DEVIL TRIES TO STOP US TODAY

The devil also gets alerted when a person starts "paying attention" to the Bible, he will make every effort to stop a person from continuing to learn and live the Word of God. He doesn't try to stop those in their ministry calling alone, but he goes after any believer who is endeavoring to learn the Word and live free from all Satan's devices.

> *...lest Satan should take advantage of us; for we are not ignorant of his devices. 2 Corinthians 2:11 NKJV*

> *"The sower sows the word. 15 And these are the ones by the wayside where the word is sown. When they hear, Satan comes immediately and takes away the word that was sown in their hearts. 16 These likewise are the ones sown on stony ground who, when they hear the word, immediately*

> *receive it with gladness; 17 and they have no root in themselves, and so endure only for a time. Afterward, when tribulation or persecution arises for the word's sake, immediately they stumble. 18 Now these are the ones sown among thorns; they are the ones who hear the word, 19 and the cares of this world, the deceitfulness of riches, and the desires for other things entering in choke the word, and it becomes unfruitful. 20 But these are the ones sown on good ground, those who hear the word, accept it, and bear fruit: some thirtyfold, some sixty, and some a hundred." Mark 4:14-20 NKJV*

This parable Jesus taught His disciples reveals the various ways a believer is stopped in their spiritual growth and victory, starting with "Satan coming immediately" to steal the Word from the hearer before it can take root as a seed in the heart. I assure you that if he can't steal the Word from the hearer, he will seek to use all the other deterrents listed in this passage to stop the believer's progress. The devil is behind it all!

When I was a new believer in 1974, I enrolled in a Community College taking a Sociology Course. I was newly Spirit filled as in Acts 2:1-4 and was super hungry for the Word of God, reading and meditating on it continually. As I mentioned earlier, I abused drugs for several years before making Jesus the Lord of my life, I smoked a lot of Pot and Hash and could recognize the smell of that smoke anytime it was in the air around me. As I travelled to College one morning, I stopped at a 7 Eleven for a coffee. Directly behind the store was a park with some young people sitting under the trees, listening to their Boom Box and smoking some "Mary Jane." When I smelled the smoke and saw them seemingly have a good time, an oppressive voice spoke to my mind saying, *"Now that you are Christian, you are not going to have any fun any more."* The devil knew that what they were doing in the park was formerly my kind of fun too. For a moment my heart sank and I started to feel sorry for myself and believed the devil's lie. Then another voice spoke clearly in my spirit, quoting a verse of Scripture I didn't know was in the Bible as of yet, He said,

> *But as it is written: "Eye has not seen, nor ear heard, Nor have entered into the heart of man The things which God has prepared for those who love Him." 10 But God has revealed them to us through His Spirit. For the Spirit searches all things, yes, the deep things of God. 1 Corinthians 2:9-10 NKJV*

Wow! When I heard those Words from the Spirit of God, the Presence of God came all over me and I began to rejoice knowing that God has just spoken to me and that the other voice of fear and discouragement was the devil trying to deceive me into backsliding. Apparently, God heard what the devil said to me and countered him with His Word. I went on my way to school with a skip in my step that has never gone away because of the joy of the Lord, and all the amazing experiences of ecstasy and delight I have experienced as I have travelled the nations with the Gospel of Jesus Christ. God plans to thrill our lives with unspeakable joy and pleasure as we walk intimately with Him.

> *You will show me the path of life; In Your presence is fullness of joy; At Your right hand are pleasures forevermore. Psalm 16:11 NKJV*

Another occasion when the devil tried to interfere with God's plan for my life, came the year before I left for Bible College in Dayton, Ohio in 1977. I was asleep in my bed when I was awoken by a very vivid dream which I will try to describe.

"I saw a staggered sidewalk of stones, except they were in the shape of crosses that glowed. Out of the dark came a pair of legs, only legs from the waist down. They were dressed in pleated trousers and wore wing tipped shoes that were "trucking over the crosses in the sidewalk." If you have ever seen those "Keep On Trucking" graphics, that is what the legs looked like, and they were pumping out joy like they had a heartbeat. I could see the joy coming out with each beat of the heart in those legs as they "trucked over the crosses."

Then I heard a voice say, *"Go the way of the cross, in it is fullness of Joy."* I sat up in my bed and was startled by it all. As I sat pondering, another voice spoke, that voice seemed like it was beside my head and it said in very oppressive voice, *"You are treading on the cross of Jesus."*

When I heard that second voice I realized it was the devil trying to deceive me because God had just spoken to me in a dream that would become a "landmark" in my life from then on. When I realized that God has shown me a path for my life, the Presence of God filled the room and I sat in bed and worshipped Him. I will tell the interpretation of that dream and how it has worked out in my life in another book, God willing.

I learned that Satan can see and hear what God

is saying and doing in the Spirit realm and will always try to distort the meaning and deceive the believer. Thank God for watching over our lives and "raising up a standard against the enemy" with His Word.

WE HAVE ADVANTAGES

What are the advantages we have over the enemy that Paul taught about in his writings to the churches? He prayed,

> *that the God of our Lord Jesus Christ, the Father of glory, may give to you the spirit of wisdom and revelation in the knowledge of Him, 18 the eyes of your understanding being enlightened; that you may know what is the hope of His calling, what are the riches of the glory of His inheritance in the saints, 19 and what is the exceeding greatness of His power toward us who believe, according to the working of His mighty power 20 which He worked in Christ when He raised Him*

from the dead and seated Him at His right hand in the heavenly places, 21 far above all principality and power and might and dominion, and every name that is named, not only in this age but also in that which is to come. 22 And He put all things under His feet, and gave Him to be head over all things to the church, 23 which is His body, the fullness of Him who fills all in all. Ephesians 1:17-23 NKJV

WE ARE NEW CREATIONS IN CHRIST.

Paul knew Jesus had authority over all the creatures existing in the demonic realm, and that he was vested with that authority as well as all believers who are ***"new creations in Christ."***

> *Therefore, if anyone is in Christ, he is a new creation; old things have passed away* (all that we were and had "in Adam")*; behold, all things have become new. 2 Corinthians 5:17 NKJV (note added)*

WE HAVE ACCESS TO ALL THE "GRACE OF GOD".

As the "body of Christ", we are "one with the Head" and can do whatever He did when on earth. Namely, "cast out devils, heal the sick and set the captives free." **We have access to all the "grace of God" that Paul had access to.**

> *Therefore, having been justified by faith, we have peace with God through our Lord Jesus Christ, 2 through whom also we have access by faith into this grace in which we stand, and rejoice in hope of the glory of God. Romans 5:1-2 NKJV*

The grace of God provides us with the nine gifts of the Holy Spirit,

> *But the manifestation of the Spirit is given to each one for the profit of all: 8 for to one is given the word of wisdom through the Spirit, to another the word of knowledge through the same Spirit, 9 to another faith by the same Spirit, to another gifts of*

healings by the same Spirit, 10 to another the working of miracles, to another prophecy, to another discerning of spirits, to another different kinds of tongues, to another the interpretation of tongues. 11 But one and the same Spirit works all these things, distributing to each one individually as He wills. 1 Corinthians 12:7-11 NKJV

ANGELIC ASSISTANCE

Are they not all ministering spirits sent forth to minister for those who will inherit salvation? Hebrews 1:14 NKJV

THE GIFT OF RIGHTEOUSNESS

For if by the one man's offense death reigned through the one, much more those who receive abundance of grace and of the gift of righteousness will reign in life through the One, Jesus Christ.) Romans 5:17 NKJV

THE AUTHORITY OF JESUS NAME

"Most assuredly, I say to you, he who believes in Me, the works that I do he will do also; and greater works than these he will do, because I go to My Father. 13 And whatever you ask in My name, that I will do, that the Father may be glorified in the Son. 14 If you ask anything in My name, I will do it." John 14:12-14 NKJV

GRACE HAS BEEN "FREELY GIVEN TO US"

There is nothing we have to "earn" by our own self effort" or performance. All things are "ours" because we are "In Christ" and must be received by faith and acted upon in order to experience their reality.

*He who did not spare His own Son, but delivered Him up for us all, how shall He not with Him also **freely** give us all things? Romans 8:32 NKJV. (emphasis added)*

> *Now we have received, not the spirit of the world, but the Spirit who is from God, that we might know the things that have been* ***freely*** *given to us by God. 1 Corinthians 2:12 NKJV (emphasis added)*

We must all pray the prayers of Paul for ourselves in order to receive the "spirit of wisdom and revelation", then Holy Spirit will open our spiritual eyes to the reality of these redemptive truths and release the power of His resurrection into our lives. We receive all that God has freely provided by faith. Faith is that which accompanies knowledge.

> *So then faith comes by hearing, and hearing by the word of God. Romans 10:17 NKJV*

As Christians we can live an overcoming life of faith when we know the truth, live humbly before God, and use the authority we have in Jesus' name. Amen.

For a more complete understanding of "New Creation Realities", I recommend my books entitled Stronger Than Satan and Victorious that are available on Amazon and johnpolis.com

STRONGER THAN SATAN

What happens when someone with authority walks into a room? They generally take charge without asking what to do. We were never meant to be in a position of asking Satan permission or direction. Believers need to walk just as Jesus walked, with boldness and authority. Jesus left us in the earth to be in charge of it, as He had intended with Adam. Satan is a dethroned ruler. He knows it, but he won't just roll over and play dead. You have to take authority over Him.

VICTORIOUS

Isaiah 54:17 says, "No weapon that is formed against thee shall prosper; and every tongue that shall rise against thee in judgment thou shalt condemn." In this book you will learn the secrets of successful spiritual warfare and defeat the giants in your life.

ENDORSEMENT: JOHN P. KELLY

Apostle John Polis's book, Victorious, is revelatory! It is a compilation of revelations on faith from scripture and the experiences of a man who lives and ministers in the faith realm. Apostle Polis recognizes that as Christians we live in an adversarial world of warfare that comes in the form of temptations, sickness, problems, conflicts, and much more. Yet, our weaponry contains a great shield of protection - the shield of faith! Victorious will equip you to live, move, and have your being within the realm of faith.

About The Author

John Polis was saved and filled with Holy Spirit in 1974 during the Jesus Movement. He attended Dayton Bible College and graduated with a B.A. in Biblical Studies in 1980, after which he became pastor of a Pentecostal church in West Virginia.

In 1983, John had an encounter that transitioned him into the ministry of Apostle. Afterwards, he began to travel as an Evangelist and International Bible Teacher.

Among the works established was Eldoret Bible College in Kenya, Africa, which was birthed in 1998 and has graduated over 2500 students with undergraduate and graduate degrees. Students have planted more than 600 churches throughout Africa to date, some of which have more than 5000 in attendance. John has been a television and radio host for more than 40 years, has authored 23 publications, and has books translated into 7 languages. As President and Founder of Revival Fellowship International, John, and his wife Rebecca, have many spiritual sons and daughters in 13 states and 5 countries. John carries and imparts an Elijah Anointing to prepare the Church for discipling nations as mature sons and daughters. John serves on the Council of Elders for the International Coalition of Apostolic Leaders and is a former United States Marine, being a veteran of the Vietnam War. John and Rebecca have been married 47 years, with 4 children and 9 grandchildren.

MORE BOOKS BY JOHN POLIS

9 Apostolic Functions:
Things Apostles Do.

Heartbeat Of An Apostle:
Revelation From The Heart Of Paul.

Built Strong:
31 Keys To Spiritual Power.

God Fathers:
How You Can Be One.

Stronger Than Satan:
Understanding Your Authority In Christ.

Victorious:
How To Face, Fight, and Finish Your Battles.

Release The River Within You:
Increasing The Anointing Flow

Put On Your Gloves:
The Five Battles Every Christian Must Win.

Apostolic Advice:
Proven Wisdom for Building Strong Foundations in the Local Church.

Recycled Believers:
Solving The Mystery of Migrating Sheep.

How To Produce Abundance In Your Life:
The Kingdom Secrets Jesus Taught His Disciples.

Biblical Headship:
Making Sense of Submission To Authority.

The Master Builder:
Wisdom for Today's Apostles

Take My Yoke Upon You:
Fulfilling Your 3 Dimensional Destiny

The Kings Are Coming:
Understanding The Kingly Anointing

BE STRONG IN THE LORD: DISCIPLESHIP SERIES BOOKS BY JOHN POLIS

Living Unshakeable In A Shaking World:
6 Principles For Successful Kingdom Living.

Total Victory Is For You:
5 Smooth Stones To Slay Your Giants.

The Love Of God

How To Obtain Strong Faith

Spiritual Warfare:
No Place For Satan

For these and additional resources to help you in your spiritual growth, go to www.johnpolis.com.

www.ingramcontent.com/pod-product-compliance
Lightning Source LLC
LaVergne TN
LVHW050609100826
845148LV00015B/3194